PRAISE FOR SISTER
SLUGGERS

"A charming novel (...ball, *Sister Sluggers* may moti   ...s to get involved in physical activities.... This funny and endearing book shows the importance of trustworthiness and repercussions of one's own actions. The heart-felt story is perfect for girls aspiring to obtain a little independence and take part in a team sport."

—Lisa Knight, *Softball West Magazine*

"*Sister Sluggers* is a great book for any softball player. Whether you're six years of age---or now a softball parent!

"This book is about two sisters who struggle with softball teams. Marianne is a pitcher, and her older sister, Emily, is a catcher. They were the first girls to use pitching signals. They were both planning on playing on the same team, but when Marianne is late for try-outs, she gets stuck on the suckiest team in the league, while her older sister, Emily, is on one of the top teams.

"This book is about the struggles that two sisters had while seperated on different teams, and how they worked together on one team. Great for any family full of ball players, or just one softball player."—Lacyn, age 11

"A wonderful story that teaches valuable lessons of teamwork and sportsmanship. Every young player should read it!"
—Kim Mouldon, *Fast Pitch Forever*

"At a time when family life seemed simpler and sibling rivalry more playful, Emily writes, in this short autobiographical tale, about her childhood days in western Massachusetts. As a close-knit family, her family is involved in many outdoor activities and sports. Among these sports, Emily and her younger sister, Marianne, pack a one-two defensive punch on the local softball team until her sister finds herself on another team.

"This is a story full of funny sibling rivalry mixed with a sad town-wide event. A good read especially for young sports-minded girls."
—Terry Dorsey, Teacher/Librarian, Fitchburg (MA) Public Schools

SISTER SLUGGERS

Emily Chetkowski

Published by:
PublishingWorks, Inc.
60 Winter Street
Exeter, NH 03833
603-778-9883

Marketing & Sales:
Revolution Booksellers, LLC
60 Winter Street
Exeter, NH 03833
1-800-REV-6603
603-772-7200

www.revolutionbooksellers.com

ISBN-13: 978-1-933002-35-4
LCCN: 2006931458

Cover Illustration by Susan Spellman
Family Photos courtesy of Emily Chetkowski
Stock Art: ENCORE Hemera Photo Clip Art 100,000
Design: Melodica Design, Exeter, NH

To Mom, the best coach, fan and cheerleader a daughter could ever have.

SISTER SLUGGERS

Emily Chetkowski

CHAPTER ONE

Where Is She?

Where is she? It's already after six o'clock. If Marianne doesn't get here soon, she's going to miss softball sign-ups! I'll bet she's doing this on purpose because she's mad at me. All I said was, I wish she'd stop following me like a shadow. I just wanted to ride my bike here alone. Well, it will serve her right if she doesn't make the team because she's late. She's being a little stinker just to make me worry. I'll see that goofy-looking yellow bike pull in here soon.

It's a good thing I showed up early to get on our team. It was filling up fast. Somehow, I don't think the Galaxies would be the same without me, their best catcher. But now it's looking like we may lose our best pitcher, my sister, Marianne. What was she thinking? How could she do this to the team? Last year, with her pitching and my catching, the Galaxies almost won the championship.

To look at us, you wouldn't know we were sisters, or that I was older. For being only 11, Marianne was pretty tall for her age, and very slim with thick, curly, black hair. A year and a half older than Mare, I was built just the opposite, short and muscular with long stick-straight brown hair.

Marianne's long arms and legs sure helped her pitching ability. Off the field, she was gangly and awkward, but on the field she elegantly used every inch of those long arms and legs to perfectly place a pitch that most batters couldn't hit.

Just as her height and leanness made her a great pitcher, my compactness made it easy to squat down behind home plate to catch those pitches. I was also quick and could maneuver easily and dive for a ball when I needed to. I had tried most of the other playing positions, but catcher suited me best.

Although physically we were total opposites, we played great together. And we were also clever.

Marianne and I were the first girls in the softball league ever to use signals to set up pitches. Believe it or not, we got the idea from making silly faces at each other. During a boring game that we were sure to win, Marianne started wiggling her eyebrows at me just before she threw the ball. I gave her a stupid look back and tried to make her laugh. And so it went for a good part of the game, but neither of us made the other one crack up. We figured no one noticed us because we didn't get in trouble. We were almost right; nobody did notice, except our Dad. Dad always noticed everything.

After the game Dad asked, "What were you two doing out there?"

"What do you mean?" I asked innocently as I quickly tried to think of a good excuse for goofing around during the game. I was hoping Mare was thinking of something too, but it was usually me who talked us out of trouble when getting in trouble was about to happen.

"Were you giving signals like Phil and Matt?"

Huh? Surprised, Mare and I just looked at each other. That thought hadn't crossed our minds but suddenly it sounded like a good idea. You see, Phil was the pitcher and Matt was the catcher on my Dad's Italian-American Vets softball team. Mare and I had often seen them using hand signals, but never really thought about it much, until now.

"Uhmm, I guess we were kind of doing that," I answered, realizing he had given us the perfect excuse and a perfect new idea. I asked Dad to explain signals to us so that we could do it right the next time. As usual, he was more than happy to. He always enjoyed teaching us something or telling us a story. Dad was a walking library.

"Okay. Then you both need to get up extra early tomorrow and be ready to work extra hard," he advised.

"You got it!" my sister said enthusiastically, but I could tell she was also enthusiastic about not getting in trouble.

"Sure, sure. Bright and early!" I promised, though I knew he would get us up way before a person should have to get up on a weekend. I preferred to sleep late on Saturdays. We didn't have games or practices on the weekends, only weeknights, so I was looking forward to relaxing a bit, but rest was not what my Dad had in mind for us.

The next morning, just as I expected, Dad got us up before the birds were even awake. Ugh. He was always so full of energy at that time of the day. Mare and I were still unconscious, but Dad had breakfast ready and big glasses of freshly squeezed orange juice. Soon we were out in the yard, semi-awake, and ready to learn signals.

Dad explained the basics. The pitcher and catcher set up the pitch to the batter with signals. The whole idea depends on being secretive though. You don't want the batter to know what kind of pitch they're going to get. The goal is to throw them off-guard so they miss the ball or hit it poorly. If the batter likes fast pitches, the pitcher might do something like touch her left ear. The catcher knows that means a slow pitch is coming, and is ready for it.

Sometimes the catcher calls the pitch. The catcher may notice that the batter is standing a little too far from the plate. She could ask the pitcher for a pitch slightly outside the strike zone, making it tough for the batter to hit it because she is standing too far away. The catcher is ready for that outside ball too, so that the pitch isn't wild which would give a runner a chance to steal a base or two.

We listened to Dad for a while then started practicing. He gave us some signal ideas, but thought it was best if we made up our own. Then he was off to a practice for his team. He had a big game later in the afternoon.

Mare and I got right to work. It wasn't as easy as we thought it would be. We couldn't agree on anything, never mind trying to remember what all the signals meant. For instance, I held up two fingers to call for a low pitch, but Mare thought I meant a fast outside one. The ball ended up way out in the woods and I had to go get it.

"Thanks a lot, Mare!" I grumbled as I worked my way through the blackberry bramble, getting all scratched up in the process.

"Pay attention next time," I said with older sister authority in my voice. The next pitch, Mare scratched the top of her left ear. Thinking that meant a high pitch, I stood up to catch it. Wrong! She threw a low pitch. The ball got me right in the shins, and I wasn't wearing shin pads. Ouch!

"Who's not paying attention, huh Em?" my bratty little sister asked. The ear scratch only meant her ear was itchy, that's all. I hadn't seen the "low pitch chin rub" signal she gave before that. We had a long way to go before we'd be game ready.

My Dad was such an avid softball player that he played for two teams: the ITAM Vets plus the town firefighters. My Dad was a volunteer fireman. Every year, the firefighters played against the town police in a Jimmy Fund benefit game. Lucky for Mare and me, the benefit game was that afternoon. Though it was always an intense game, the firefighters usually won. When it came to softball, the police and the firemen were fierce competitors.

The game was always a big family event and

my whole family attended. Mom and my two older sisters watched and cheered. Mare and I watched too, but that day we watched even more carefully. We wanted to play just like Dad and his friends and we studied their every move.

Wow, were Matt and Phil good! Sometimes you could hardly tell they were signaling to each other. Mare and I studied them and tried to figure out the signals, but it was tough. We decided to be as tricky as they were.

That Sunday afternoon, after sleeping later than the day before, we practiced like crazy—pitch after pitch, signal after signal. Eventually, we got pretty good. At first, we kept our signals simple, then we started to add some tricky ones, like pretending to brush dirt off my knee with my index finger pointing at the ground to call for an inside low pitch. We even used a few of those funny faces we made at the last game. We were actually having fun now. I was eager to try it all out, but our game the next day was against the Satellites. The Satellites were a tough team to beat and there wouldn't be any room for error.

"So, what do you think Mare? Want to try it tomorrow?" I asked my sister after we finished practicing. I wondered if we should try something so new, especially against a good team.

"I don't know, Em. Think it will work?" she replied.

"How do I know? But hey, if it doesn't work,

we'll just stop before we lose too badly," I said.

"Let's give it a try then," she said as she put her glove down and walked away to get something cold to drink.

We didn't tell anyone about our plan, not even our coach because we didn't want the Satellites to find out in any way, shape, or form.

That next day, to the unaware, our subtle moves and silly faces looked like we were just being goofy. But we were dead serious, and our efforts sure paid off. Marianne was striking out just about everyone who walked up to that plate! She threw all kinds of pitches: low, high, fast, slow, inside, outside, you name it. The batters were caught off guard. They didn't know what to expect next, and we were winning the game. Things went just as we had planned. If I noticed the batter standing too close to the plate, I'd signal for a fast inside ball. Then I'd hold my catcher's mitt a bit inside.

"No hitter here, easy out Mare," I'd say to get the batter flustered. Mare would aim for my mitt as a target. Standing too close to the plate, the batter couldn't hit the ball, though the pitch was still within the strike zone.

"Steeerrriiiiiike!" the umpire would call out. Oh, how I loved to hear that word! It was great, until the other team's coach got suspicious. Mr. Richards had been watching us carefully. He happened to be one of the policemen that my Dad's firefighter's team had just beaten badly.

"Time out," Mr. Richards said assertively, holding his arm up in the air as he walked over to the umpire.

Mr. Richards talked and the ump listened. Our coach, Mr. Cushman, came trotting over to home plate to join the conversation. I stepped back and listened, too. Mr. Richards was mad and he was mad about our signals. He said they weren't allowed in our softball league. Coach Cushman was clueless. He had no idea what was going on. So, of course, he denied we were using them. Then they called Mare and me over to the plate. We were nervous.

"Just a quick question, girls. Were you using hand signals to set up your pitches?" the umpire asked.

I glanced at Mare, she glanced back at me. Her eyes said "Uh oh." Then I looked at the coaches and the ump. I knew right away what we had to say.

"Yes, we were," I replied sheepishly.

In a flash, the rulebook for our 8 to 12-year-old softball league appeared in the umpire's hand. Though the ump couldn't find any rules about signals in the book, he decided that we couldn't use them anymore, and let the game continue. Mare and I had never intended to cause a problem. We felt bad about the whole thing. Our coach was smart, though. Mr. Cushman knew we had something here and he wasn't going to give up so easily. I saw him go over to talk to Coach Richards for a few more minutes. He was smiling when he called Mare and me over to him after that inning finished.

I've got a plan," he said. "We're going to hold a meeting tomorrow night to discuss this. Mr. Richards just made a stink because he's a sore loser. I'm pretty sure I can talk the other coaches into allowing the use of signals."

Mare and I looked at each other in amazement. This was incredible. They were having a meeting just because of us. Cool! We were fired up when we returned to the game and managed to win even without using signals. We had really psyched out the Satellites.

Mr. Richards didn't look happy when he left the field that evening. I heard him grumbling something about "just like their old man," but I'm not quite sure what he meant. We heard that Coach Cushman was pretty convincing at that special meeting. He must have been, because the other coaches voted to allow signals. There was one problem with that, though: now every team was going to be using them. Still, we were flattered to be such trendsetters. That didn't stop Mare and me, however. We stuck with it and changed our secret signals for every game so that no one could figure them out. It was hard work remembering the new signals all the time, but not that bad as long as I was sure to wear my full catcher's gear when we practiced. Better to have the ball bounce off my shin pads than my shins.

The other teams were not quite as clever. Their signals were so obvious that Mare and I easily caught on to what they meant and were able to warn our teammates before they went to bat. We knew what kind of pitch was coming. It was easy to set up and get ready for it, and we hit a lot of pitches that way. Before long, the Galaxies were the team to watch out for and Mare and I were the talk of the league. We felt important. Not only had we introduced signals to our league, but also we were the best at it. The other teams dreaded playing us and we ate that up!

Our team didn't win the championship that season, but we sure came close. The game wasn't only about pitching and catching; batting and field-work counted as well, and our team still needed work in those areas. There was always next year.

Now here it is next year already, with the new season about to start. My sister and I have been hard at work practicing on our own after school. As soon as the snow thawed, we started riding our bikes to build up endurance. We just knew this was our year to win and we were going to be ready. No more second place for the Galaxies. Oooh, but that sister of mine! She could be so good, then the next minute so unreliable. Sign-ups are almost over and still no Marianne. She probably stopped to get penny candy or something. If only I had agreed to take the tandem bike here tonight like she had wanted to, then she'd be here right now. But when she had asked me to, I was not in the mood to be stuck with her on a bicycle-built-for-two, especially after her last little prank on that bike...

The "tandem-bike incident," was one of my sister's most memorable pranks. It was one I would rather forget. It happened one evening when Mare and I decided to ride the bike to Tehan's Store. Mare was pedaling in back and I was pedaling up front. I was busy talking, telling Mare some story or whatever. We rode past our friend Debbie's house. Debbie lived on the Main Road, about halfway to the store. I was still talking as we started up the big hill, just before the store. Suddenly I noticed that Marianne was awfully quiet, and the bike was awfully hard to pedal, like I was the only one pedaling.

"Hey, Mare," I said, but got no response.

"Mare?" I said again as I glanced back over my shoulder, expecting to see my sister, but I didn't! Marianne was gone! Shocked, I almost spilled the bike as I quickly turned around and headed back to look for her, pedaling that big heavy bike like crazy. I slowed to look in every ditch, thinking she'd fallen off and gotten hurt.

"Mare! Mare!" I called out her name as I searched along the side of the road for her. I couldn't stop thinking that if only I'd been listening instead of talking, I might have heard her fall off!

I rode like mad all the way back to Debbie's house. And lo and behold there she was, standing with Debbie in her driveway, both of them laughing their faces off at me! That little stinker had secretly jumped off the bike way back when we rode by Debbie's house!

"Ha ha," she laughed. "You dummy," my sister said, with tears in her eyes from laughing so hard. "Did you go all the way to Tehan's?"

She and Debbie thought it was funny, but I sure didn't. I must have looked weird riding down Main Street on a bicycle-built-for-two, all alone, talking to myself! I was a bit upset as I threw the bike down on the grass.

"You ride this all by yourself and see how you like it," I snarled as I started to walk the rest of the way home.

From then on I avoided the tandem bike and any further humiliation. But now I almost wished I'd given in instead of waiting and wondering where the heck she'd gone.

CHAPTER TWO

An Attempted Save

I hated to do it, but if Mare was going to make the team this year, I needed to bail her out. I really didn't have a choice. She was her own worst enemy and looking out for her was my lot in life. Mom was always saying, "Well, you're her big sister, and you need to set a good example for her." It would be nice if just once Marianne would learn from that example.

While trying to think up an excuse for her, I walked over to Mr. Cushman, our same coach as last year. He was very involved with girl's softball, probably because he had five daughters of his own, but he was also a great coach.

We were a "softball family," too. Both of our older sisters used to play at one time. Donna, the oldest, was now 18, but when she was my age she was a decent player. She usually played third base because she could stop anything and she had an incredible throwing arm. Unfortunately, at times, her aim and accuracy left much to be desired, especially when she threw to first base. As long as the first baseman could jump high and had a great reach, everything was fine. Nevertheless, Donna did in a few first basemen.

Donna was an exceptionally fast base runner and scored a lot of runs. Her specialty was stealing bases. She was good at it, especially after Dad taught her how to slide, which she could somehow do without getting dirty. That was Donna—

she hated getting dirt on her clothes and usually managed not to, even in the game of softball.

Dad says that Donna hates dirt because Mom always dressed her in pretty white dresses when she was little. Donna loved to have tea parties and act like a princess. Every picture I ever saw of her when she was small showed her in a frilly dress at some social event. She was always a lady no matter what she wore, even if it was a softball uniform.

Once, when Donna was four years old, my Dad was taking care of her while Mom was out shopping with her friends. Donna was wearing one of her fancy dresses as usual. My Dad had plans for them that day, but it wasn't a tea party. He was going to teach her how to be a bit outdoorsier for a change. Donna, however, wouldn't change out of that pretty dress no matter what, but that didn't stop my Dad. He taught her how to make mud pies anyway, white dress and all. Donna loved playing in the mud so much that day that her pretty white dress was no longer pretty and no longer white. My Dad tried to wash it before my mother found out, but he got caught when she came home a bit earlier than expected. Fortunately, my mother had come home from shopping with yet another pretty dress for Donna.

Over time, my Dad managed to bring out the athlete in Donna, and she was the one who inspired all of us girls to play softball. Donna loved to play and we loved to go to all her games and cheer her on.

My other older sister was a sports star as well. Joanne played catcher, but she usually got a bad case of pre-game jitters. She was always saying she wanted to quit and that this was going to be her last game ever, until the game got underway. Then it was a different story. She was a serious player, even though her catching equipment was too big and made her look like a turtle. At least that was what our grandfather said. He loved to tease her about that. Actually, Grandpa liked to tease all of us about everything!

I remember when I was just starting to play ball. Dad and I were out in the yard playing catch. He was throwing the ball way up in the air for me to catch just like a pop-up fly ball. Getting that ball to stay in my glove did not come naturally to me. I was a total klutz.

"Em," Dad said. "Put your other hand over the ball when it lands in your glove. That way you'll have it for sure," he advised.

Grandpa was on the porch watching us. I could hear him chuckling at every ball I missed, which was just about every throw. Next thing I know, here comes Grandpa out of the garage, grinning from ear to ear, carrying a huge peach basket. (Grandpa loved to go fruit picking, especially peaches and strawberries.)

"Here Aimily," (as he used to call me), "maybe this will help," Grandpa said with a mischievous twinkle in his eye as he handed me the bushel basket. Dad fell on the ground cracking up with laughter.

A few days later, after one of my first softball games, I came home all excited.

"Grandpa, guess what? I said breathlessly.

"What?" he replied.

"My coach says I'm the fastest runner on the team!" I was so proud of myself.

"Well, I'd sure hate to see the slowest!" Grandpa said with that twinkle in his eye again. Looking at the silly smirk on Grandpa's face, it was easy to tell who Marianne got her mischievous streak from. But I knew Grandpa was proud of me. He was just a big kidder and I adored him, even when he purposely hid the comic section of the Sunday paper and told me they must not have printed them that week. The funny pages were easy to find, however; usually behind the wing chair in the living room. That was where he sometimes hid the dozen honey-dipped and Boston Creme donuts he brought us too. He always bought us our favorites and we always knew where he hid them. Even though he did this more often than not, we played along. Grandpa had a big heart but he liked to make everyone laugh more than anything.

Catching is an important position, but not many people realize it. When a catcher gets to make a play, it's usually a crucial one. I thought it was neat to watch my sister Joanne catch a pop-up foul ball to make an easy out, sometimes saving the game. To Joanne there was nothing better than stopping a run at home plate. But to the runners, there was nothing worse than heading in to score only to find Joanne standing there holding the ball waiting to tag them out. The runners knew they were doomed. There was just no getting by my sister Joanne and those plays always made the crowd go nuts. It could be a rough position to play, though. Joanne got hit with foul tips and bad pitches more often than not, and runners would smash into her trying to make it home. Many times she had to scramble in the dirt to retrieve a wild pitch before any bases were stolen. By the end of a game, Joanne would be totally covered with dirt and dust. (It was a good that Mom had tired of the frilly white dress thing after Joanne had been born.) Luckily, she was nothing like Donna. To be a good catcher, you can't worry about a little dirt.

Even after seeing all this, I wanted to be just like my sister Joanne. I wanted to be a catcher. Watching our older sisters and our Dad play was probably why Mare and I just naturally signed up for the league when we were old enough, which was 8 to 12 in our town. I don't remember anyone ever questioning whether we were going to do it or not. We just did it. Softball was in our blood. By the time I started playing, my older sisters had quit the game. They were more interested in other things, like going out with boys and going to the mall to buy the clothes to wear when going out with the boys. All their friends were the same way, too. It seemed dumb to me, but I guess that's what you did when you were their age.

I have always had bigger plans, though. Next year, when I turn 13, if I am good enough, I will be eligible for the teen girl's softball travel team. I had that to think about, not weird boys with pimples!

Now everything was in jeopardy because of Marianne; I needed to act fast.

"Mr. Cushman," I said after I finally got his undivided attention. "Marianne was right behind me on her bike. She must have gotten a flat tire or something. One did look like it needed air. Want me to go look for her?" I asked.

It was the best excuse I could think of now. I hated to lie but I thought it would be worse to say the truth: she wasn't there because she was being a little jerk.

"Well, I can't hold her place any longer. I have to be fair to the others," he answered with a frown on his face. "I'll see if someone else has room for her so she at least gets in the league this year," he said while he looked at the sign-up sheet.

I understood. Everyone wanted a chance to be on the Galaxies. Coach Cushman had been patient long enough.

Seven P.M! That's what time Marianne finally showed up at Mapleshade Field. Annoyed, I pretended not to see her. She ignored me, too. I just wish I could have seen the look on her face when she found out she was signed up for the Comets, the only team with a position left and the worst one in the league. They didn't win a single game the previous year. Hah! It served her right!

CHAPTER THREE
Family!

"Emily, where's Marianne?" Mom was busy doing laundry.

I shrugged my shoulders.

"Didn't you girls come home together?" she asked. But I didn't need to answer her. She took one look at my fed-up expression and figured it out for herself. "OK, now what happened?" said Mom as she sorted socks.

"Well, the little creep really did it this time! We were on Elm Street and she was riding her bike right on my tail. I told her to quit it and to stop asking me so many silly questions. 'Who's that you waved to Em? Do you think we'll make it on time? Is it true that Nancy Partridge shaves her legs already?' Blah, blah, blah. She was just really bugging me." I walked over to the sink to get a cold drink of water.

"And?" My mother wanted to hear the rest of the story.

"Oh," I replied. "Well, Miss Sensitive got mad at me of course, took off somewhere, then showed up too late to make the team. Now she has to play on the Comets, and I don't really care!" I folded my arms across my chest.

Shaking her head, Mom said, "Oh, you girls. You don't know how lucky you are."

Oh, no, here we go again, I thought. This would bring on the "When I was your age" speech.

"When I was your age, I never argued with my sister. She was all I had after my mother died. We were best friends. You don't need to be best friends, but is it so much to ask for the both of you to just try to get along?" Mom looked flustered.

I had heard this speech sooo many times before, but I had learned to tune her out and still look like I was listening.

"Now get going and find her," she added with her hands on her hips.

"Okay, okay, I'm going" I replied as I headed for the door.

"And while you're at it, apologize. I'm sure Marianne's feelings are hurt." Mom just had to add that.

Well, I couldn't help it—Mom's words stuck in my head. I started to feel a little guilty. So, I headed out the door, across the backyard, and past the pool until I came to the edge of the woods that surrounded our house. There were a lot of woods back there, but I had a good idea of where she was. Before I headed into the woods, I picked up an acorn cap that had lost its nut.

"Ssshhhhrrreeeeee." I stopped and used it as a whistle to call her so she'd know I was looking for her.

Marianne and I were the only ones around who could whistle with an acorn. It was really an easy thing to do, once you got the hang of it. All you had to do was hold the cap between and behind your slightly bent thumbs in just the right way, purse your lips, rest your bottom lip against your knuckles, then blow. The shrill whistle could be very loud if you knew what you were doing, and I did.

"SSSHHHHHHRRRRREEEEEEEE," I whistled again, much louder than the first time.

Great. No answer. She's going to make me come get her. If Mom hadn't made me feel so bad I wouldn't bother to look any further, but Mom was good at that. I set off down the path and toward the pond. It was only a two-minute walk, but it was a whole world away and my favorite place to go.

"Hey Pemplepee, what took you so long?" There she was, sitting in my favorite hiding place by the pond, just as I figured. Oh, how I hated it when she called me that stupid name! I had no idea what it meant; she made it up one day and it just stuck.

This was my special place, a little shady nook right by the stream that lead off from the pond. I liked to come here to think or when I needed to be by myself. The sights and sounds were so soothing. But it was my spot, not hers, and Mare was sitting here purposely trying to annoy me. And she was really getting on my nerves!

"Quit calling me that," I said. "Didn't you hear me whistle?"

"No," she replied.

Oh, right! I knew she had heard me, but just didn't care.

"Well, you better go home and tell Mom you're okay. She's the one who's looking for you, not me."

I didn't want to admit that I was feeling a little guilty.

The pond was a beautiful place. I often saw ducks, turtles, and all kinds of birds there. I loved to hear the peepers in the spring and the big bullfrogs croak in the summer. In the winter, my sisters and I and our friends ice skated on the pond. Sometimes, a bunch of boys would try to hog the whole thing to play hockey, but there just wasn't enough room on that pond for all of us. Mare and I usually managed to take back the ice, however. We were good at getting in their way or ultimately hiding the puck, especially if we were the ones who shoveled off all the snow in the first place.

"What's wrong Pemps? Are you mad at me? I thought you'd be happy to have me off the team," said Marianne as she turned over some rocks to look for salamanders.

"Why should I be mad? I showed up on time and made the team. What are you going to say when everyone asks how come you're on the Comets this year? Don't expect me to make up an excuse for you. I'll just tell them it's because you're a little stinker, that's all," I replied. "And I said to quit calling me that!"

I pitched my acorn cap into the pond, pretending a cattail plant was my batter up.

"Low, inside," my sister said.

"Of course it is, an acorn shell is too light to pitch," I said as I picked up a rock and pitched again. This time I almost hit a red-winged blackbird that was clinging to another cattail. It squawked and sputtered off to a safer spot across the pond.

"Maybe you should just stick to catching," my sister remarked, laughing.

"Maybe you should just get going, Mare. I think I heard Mom calling you." Not really, but there was no sense in being humiliated any further.

Pitching was the only position I wasn't good at, but I still wanted to try it sometime. Mare was a natural at it. She knew I envied her ability and liked to rub it in whenever she had a chance.

"Oh, yah and I'm supposed to be sorry for hurting your feelings." I didn't really mean it but I needed to smooth things over before she got home or Mom would be on my case again.

"Don't worry, you didn't hurt my feelings, PEM-PLEPEE!" Then my little sister smiled that silly smile of hers and turned up the path, headed home.

CHAPTER FOUR

I Wish I Were an Only Child

My friend Kim definitely had it made. She was just sitting around watching TV when I called. Lucky her, with no brothers or sisters to drive her crazy, she gets to watch whatever shows she wants to. Plus, she has her parents all to herself and they totally spoil her. She gets to do a lot of neat stuff without a little sister tagging along.

Kim is my best friend, but I should have known she'd take Marianne's side when I told her the latest. Whenever I complain about my sister, Kim always defends her. Then, to make me feel worse, she tells me how lonely it can get being an only child, and she doesn't spare any words.

"Oh, Emily, stop complaining. I wish I had a sister to do stuff with," Kim said, just as I expected. See, I shouldn't have bothered to tell her.

"Well, if you did have a sister, she'd probably be nice and not anything like Marianne," I said. "I'll tell you what—maybe one day we should trade places. Then you'd see what it's like to live with her," I replied, rather pleased with myself. Kim has no clue!

"Don't get me wrong. I think what Mare did tonight was pretty dumb, too," said Kim. Finally, someone sees my side for a change. "But Emily, you've done some terrible stuff to her," she reminded.

"I've never done anything as bad as what she did today," I said.

"That's what you think. How about when she got her new bike? You told me it wasn't fair because blue was your favorite color, not hers. I just knew it was you who talked Marianne into spray-painting it that awful school bus yellow," Kim said.

She was annoyingly right.

"Well, yellow is her favorite color. She even spray painted the tires yellow and loved it!" I replied. "Besides, it's not my fault if she's dumb enough to do anything anybody tells her to do," I said.

Marianne rides that yellow spray-painted bike everywhere. Everybody likes to tease her about it, but she pretends not to care. She has never once admitted that it looks stupid. I actually think she is kind of proud of it.

Dad had worked overtime to buy that bike for her. As the youngest of four children, Marianne was always getting the hand me down stuff at its worst. I guess Dad felt bad about that. I just wished that he had felt bad for me. I had my sister Joanne's old bike and it was pretty beat up. No one offered to buy me a new bike of any color.

I remember that it was especially hot the day that we painted Marianne's bike. We were think-ing about clothes-pinning playing cards on our spokes and riding by Old Man Roberts house to bug him, but it was just too hot. Old Man Rob-erts lived on the next street in a run-down house with junk all over the yard. His house was next to the swamp and we were told that muskrats and snapping turtles would come out and bite us if we went too close. It was rumored that Old Man Roberts had fistfuls of gold coins hidden under the floorboards of his house, and the house was haunted. We were told he lived there alone and talked to spirits. He was rich, but creepy.

Sometimes, we would bravely ride our bikes by his house, but never alone. It was the shortest route to Debbie's, and we avoided traffic by going that way. And sometimes we could see him peeking out the window from behind a torn, dirty curtain. We would scream and pedal faster!

One day, Debbie's father taught us how to put playing cards on our bike spokes with clothespins to make a neat snapping sound as we rode. It was a blast until we decided to take the shortcut back home past Old Man Roberts' house. We took a right onto Voyer Avenue, just around the corner from Debbie's. As Mare and I got closer to Old Man Roberts' house, we looked to see if he was watching us in the window, but he wasn't.

Suddenly, just as we were passing his front door, he came running out of the house chasing after us, yelling and waving his arms over his head! He was just as scary as we had imagined—all wrinkly with a scruffy beard. His clothes were shabby and dirty, but worst of all he was angry!

"You kids get out of here with that noise! I

can't stand that noise!" he yelled at us like a crazy man.

And get out of there we did! But fast! We never pedaled so hard in our lives, screaming the whole way home. Soon, word got out about Old Man Roberts chasing us. Everyone avoided using Voyer Avenue for a while, but eventually a bunch of us decided that we weren't going to let him scare us like that. We would go that way regardless. Besides, it was too dangerous to ride on the main road with all the traffic.

Riding by his house became kind of a dare. We'd wait on our bikes at the bottom of the hill near his house. Then, we would take turns, bravely riding up as close as we dared while our friends held their breath watching, ready to take off in a flash. Not much happened until one day some of our friends boldly rode by with cards in their spokes. Once again, Old Man Roberts came out yelling. Even though everyone eventually had their turn at taunting and being chased by the old man, we were still afraid of him and his haunted house.

The day we painted Marianne's bike, it was just too hot to do anything but pick on each other. Marianne kept teasing me because my bike was old and hers was so shiny. I said her bike color was ugly and nobody rode blue bikes anyway. In reality, it was the most beautiful bike I had ever seen.

For some strange reason she agreed with me

and decided she should change the color. We went into the garage to see what other colors we might find to paint it. Mare was thrilled when we found the can of spray paint called School Bus Yellow. She said it was her favorite color and we got busy creating our masterpiece. We ran out of paint just about the time that Dad came home from work. He saw us in the garage, but he was too late. The terrible deed was done. Every inch of that bike was screaming yellow. Dad just stood there, tired and sweaty, staring at the bike. It seemed like his whole body just went limp. He was totally speechless, which was probably lucky for us. He didn't need to say a thing. I knew what that look on his face meant, I wouldn't be getting a new bike anytime soon.

"How about the time you told her to throw stones at that huge yellow jacket nest in your yard?" Kim said rather critically. "Marianne got stung all over and so did your Mom trying to rescue both of you. That was bright, Em!"

I could tell it was time to end this conversation.

"I got stung a couple of times, too, you know," I said in defense. Actually, I was only stung twice but Mom and Mare each had at least a dozen bites.

There was a HUGE yellow jacket nest near the stonewall, at the edge of our driveway. Mom warned both of us to stay away from it.

Dad planned to get rid of it after he came home from work. That was fine, but it meant that we couldn't ride our bikes or even play basketball in the driveway. Then, I had this brilliant idea. I would get Marianne to smash the nest with a rock so that the wasps would leave to find a new home! Good idea! Wrong. Marianne picked up a couple of rocks, and, with her incredible aim, hit the bull's-eye with her first shot.

"BZZZZZZZZZZZZZZZZ . . ." Wow, I had never seen so many wasps! They swarmed around the damaged nest then turned and started to chase us! There must have been at least a hundred angry wasps after us! I took off, running like crazy, and made it to the house before Marianne did.

Quickly, I opened the door, went in, and locked it, leaving Mare outside. Bees were swarming around her and I didn't want them in the house. Mom heard the screaming and came to her rescue while I stood safely behind the screen door. I watched in horror as Mom swatted the bees with a dishtowel and pulled Mare back into the house.

My mother was as angry as one of those bees. My two stings were nothing compared to all the bites Mom and Mare got. Mare told her it was all my idea, and I didn't get to watch TV for a week.

"Well, anyway, I've got to go now. I'll see you at practice on Monday," I said to Kim. And with that, I hung up the phone.

I was glad Kim didn't bring up the time I talked Marianne into putting things up her nose. It happened a few years earlier, but Kim knew all about it. I have no idea why I told Marianne to do it, but worse than that was: Why in the world did she listen to me all the time?

We were sitting on the lawn one pretty spring day, looking for four-leaf clovers, but not having any luck. Suddenly, my sister found these little brown oval-shaped things that looked like raisins. We couldn't tell what they were. However, I thought that I had the perfect solution on how to figure it out. I told my sister to pick them up and smell them.

Carefully, she picked them up, held them about six inches from her nose and took a whiff.

"I don't smell anything," she said.

"That's because you are holding them too far away," I said, always the authority. "Hold them closer to your nose, Mare."

So, she moved them a few inches closer to her nose.

"Still don't smell anything," she said.

"Closer," I said more convincingly.

Watching her, I was reminded of the Thanksgiving when our cousin Donny stuck extra large pitted olives in his nostrils to be funny.

"Nope, can't smell a thing," Mare said once more after she moved them within an inch of her nostrils.

"Put them up your nose!" I suggested as kind of a dare.

Well, unbelievably, Mare did it! She put the squishy brown balls right up her nose! Then, just like my cousin's olives, they got stuck. Only these were smaller than the olives and they went up farther! I ran in the house to get Mom.

"Marianne!" she said in horror. "Why in the world did you put rabbit turds up your nose?"

I looked at Mare in disgust. Rabbit turds?!? Gross! I wondered if she could smell them now or worse yet, taste them!

"Get them out!" my sister screamed.

"Hurry up Mom," I said, feeling queasy. But getting them out of her nose was no simple task. First, Mom tried to pull them out with tweezers, but that didn't work. Then, in desperation, she returned from the kitchen with a fork. It looked scary to me, but the fork worked—just in time, too. Mom was about ready to take Mare to the hospital to have a doctor remove them.

Poor Marianne. She kept blowing her nose and spitting all afternoon. I didn't dare ask her if she ever smelled them or not. In fact, we never talked about the rabbit-turd incident again. Thank goodness my Mom was quick thinking.

Sometimes I wonder how she survived our childhood years.

CHAPTER FIVE

Time to Get Serious

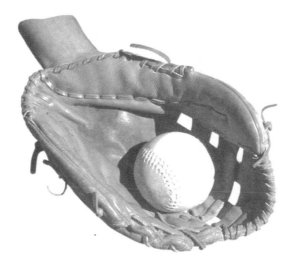

Only two more weeks of school until summer vacation, but softball season was already in full swing. With practices nearly every evening, it seemed like school would never end. I was anxious to make playing softball and going to the beach my number one priorities.

The Galaxies were looking good, even though we were all a little rusty at first. Coach Cushman wanted us to try playing different positions this year, everyone except me. He said I was his best catcher and he wanted to keep me there. Too bad, I was hoping to get a shot at my sister's vacant pitching position, mostly just to torment her.

It was also obvious that Mare had been our best pitcher. Actually, she was our only pitcher. No one on our team even came close. Coach ended up trying out just about everyone to take her place, or at least it sure seemed like it. Nobody could throw a ball anywhere near my glove, no matter what I did. With every wild pitch, I got a mouthful of dirt scrambling for it, and often a bruise or two. I finally stopped trying so hard to catch the ball and focused more on saving my life. It wasn't easy.

Coach finally decided who the team pitchers would be and found everyone else a suitable position. Then the fine-tuning began. Practice. Practice. Practice. I had a lot of work to do if I was going to whip these new pitchers into shape before the real games started. Still, we were all making a good team effort and practicing extra hard.

Mare and I played catch at home, even though we were on opposing teams. I felt bad for her, what with being on the Comets and all, and I felt a little like it was my fault. I must admit, I really missed having her on my team this year. Our pitchers were improving, but I never felt a connection with any of them like there had been when Mare was pitching. She and I just clicked out there.

Games started as scheduled. Our first was against the Saturns and it was a difficult one, mostly due to bad out-fielding and wild pitches. I really got beat up behind the plate! That game was close, but we managed to win by one run. The next few games weren't easy either, but they should have been. We needed to get our act together, even though we were somehow winning.

As I expected, the Comets were having a tough time of it and Marianne was struggling, too. One day I stopped to watch one of her games on the way home from my practice. Mare looked awkward on the mound and it seemed like the catcher would rather daydream than play softball. Then Coach Sullivan decided to pull Marianne. She went over and sat on the bench with her head down, kicking at a little stone. I could see she was pouting, too, even though she was trying to hide it.

Mary Beth, one of our new pitchers, stopped to watch with me.

"Wow, I'm kind of glad she's not on our team this year. She's awful," she said, thinking she was far superior.

"Yah, it serves her right," I said. But deep down

inside I felt very sad for my little sister. She hadn't seen me yet and I didn't want her to know I was watching. I got back on my bike and headed home.

"Well, she's learning a lesson," I thought to myself and toughened up as I rode away.

Playing softball and going to the beach with Mom and Grandpa were all we did during that summer. My parents owned a house at the seashore and we went there whenever it wasn't rented. Our softball schedule was usually convenient—no games or practices on weekends—but sometimes we missed a game when we were at the beach during vacation.

Our house was a two-minute walk to the beach. At McCook's Point Park, there were swings, see-saws, and a rocky shore to climb on and explore. Early one morning Marianne and I headed to the point to go bottom fishing off the rocks. Occasionally, we caught flounder there, but mostly we caught spider crabs and an eel or two.

That day, Marianne got a bite the minute her lure hit the water.

"I got a bite! A big one," Mare cried out.

"Pull it in, pull it in!" I said. By the way her pole was bending, I could tell it was something HUGE.

She struggled and finally landed it. When we saw what it was, we were petrified. It was the weirdest thing we had ever seen and just plain UGLY! We had no idea what kind of fish creature it was. It was big and puffed up like a blowfish and had spikes all over its body. Plus it had big sharp teeth. Every time we went near it, the thing hissed at us!

"What should we do with it?" Marianne asked.

I had no idea, but I knew I sure wasn't going to touch it. In fact, it was too ugly to even talk Marianne into touching it. After a lot of discussion, we decided to just cut the line and throw it back in—hook, line, and sinker. I cut and Marianne threw. We had the willies the whole day after seeing that fish.

Afterwards, we went up to the huge maple tree that grew on the point. It was very old, but the hundreds of initials that were carved in its bark were what made it unique. Mare and I spent the rest of the morning trying to figure out whose initials they were. Then we saw them: inside a freshly carved heart were the initials "DD & WB" Those were our sister Donna and her boyfriend's initials! We decided to walk over to Hole in the Wall Beach, which was right next to the park. All the older kids went to this beach. Our parents didn't allow Mare and I to go there, but there was a tree nearby we could climb to spy on them.

We climbed that tree and looked for Donna and her boyfriend. Sure enough there they were, holding hands! We took off for home to tell Mom. When we got there, we told Mom the news but she didn't react like we expected.

"Someday, a boy might carve your initials in that tree, you know," she said.

My sister and I just looked at each other a bit surprised. Was that a good thing or a bad thing?

Well, knowing boys, we figured it must be bad. At that moment, we decided we'd better check that tree for our initials frequently. That way, we could figure out who it was that liked us and stay as far away from them as possible!

We didn't have much use for boys; most we knew were a nuisance. They liked to tease us about playing softball, saying things like it was an easy girl's game and it didn't compare to baseball. But Mare and I got a chance to prove them wrong that summer when they asked us to play in their game when they were short players one day. We hesitated to accept their offer at first. We had asked them if we could play so many times before, but they wouldn't let us because we were girls. Now they were desperate. We thought about being mean and not helping out, but we just couldn't pass up a chance to play.

Of course, they stuck us out in left and right field, far away from the action. But because Mare and I played so well, it wasn't long before we were switched to the infield. We were batting great too and in the end, our side won. Predictably, those boys asked us to play in a few more games, but we put our noses up in the air and declined.

CHAPTER SIX
Sister Shenanigans

Mare and I were getting along pretty well, most of the time, anyway. Maybe being on different teams was really a good thing. Although my sister struggled to keep her pitching position on her new team, she often ended up in the outfield, partly because the coach liked to put his daughter on the mound. I didn't tease her about it. I didn't have to. I knew how much she hated playing the outfield. I was struggling too. Mare and I had pretty much the same problem to deal with. We just did not have the same pitcher/catcher connection with our new teammates that we had with each other.

My team's standings were good, though. We were one of the top teams. Surprisingly, so was Marianne's team. The Galaxies needed to keep an eye on them for sure. They were quietly catching up to us.

Soon the day arrived when the Galaxies and Comets had to play each other. I was more worried about losing the game, than the rivalry between my sister and me. Getting beat by her team would be more humiliating than getting beat by my little sister, but my worries were unnecessary. Marianne's team played like the same old clumsy Comets and we scored like crazy. Mare had been stuck out in left field for most of the game, until her coach decided to let her pitch near the end. She managed to put a stop to our lucky streak, but by then it was too late for them to catch up.

I didn't get it. How could the Comets be ranked

as one of the top teams? The only thing they had going for them was my sister's pitching, that is, when her coach realized this fact and let Mare pitch instead of his own daughter.

After the game, I looked for Marianne, but her team was having a meeting with their coach. I didn't feel like waiting. Besides, she was probably pouting and mad at me because my team won. She wouldn't want to ride her bike home with me anyway, so I set off without her.

I was halfway home when Marianne came out of nowhere on that unmistakable yellow bike. She went flying by, not even looking at me. I could see that pout on her face a mile away, but what I saw next surprised the daylights out of me. The back of her bike didn't look yellow anymore—it looked blue again! I tried to catch up with her to get a better look, but she was really moving and obviously in a bad mood.

When I got home, I went out to the garage to see what she had done to her bike. I was right, the back fender had hardly any yellow paint left on it. It actually looked almost new again. Interesting. Still, the rest of the bike was screaming yellow.

"Mom, has Dad been fixing up Mare's bike? It's starting to look blue again," I asked when I went back in the house.

"No, Dad hasn't touched it. Marianne has. She's been carefully using steel wool to rub the yellow paint off. She's doing a pretty good job, don't you think?" Mom said, busy cooking as usual.

"I guess so." I was a bit surprised, but I didn't want to react too much. Who knew what Mare was really up to.

"Hey, can I have Kim over tonight?" I asked. It was Friday, our usual night for TV and popcorn.

"Mare already has Judy coming over, but I guess it's okay, just as long as you leave them alone."

Now that was a twist: me leaving them alone. Try the other way around, Mom.

"And whatever you do, don't tease her about her game today," warned Mom. "I don't want any problems tonight."

Believe me, I did not intend to say a thing. I knew well enough to stay away from Marianne when she was in a bad mood. I wasn't a dummy.

Kim came over later that evening. We were craving something chocolate, so we decided to make brownies instead of our usual popcorn. Marianne and Judy were in Mare's room listening to tapes, or so we thought. Dad wasn't home yet; he had to work late.

"I'll take them out Mom," I said when the oven timer went off.

"Be careful—don't get burned," she warned.

Kim and I couldn't wait until the brownies cooled so we could eat them. They smelled so good and we were starved. Suddenly, we heard a loud thud outside and then footsteps running off into the dark. Mom quickly turned on the outside lights.

"Look!" Kim said, startled. "The wood pile is knocked over."

"Mom, someone must be out there!" I said, scared to death. It was creepy to think that someone had been just outside the kitchen window.

"Ok, don't get upset. It's probably nothing, but I'll call the police to have them look around," she said reassuringly, as she reached for the phone and dialed. "Don't say anything to Mare and Judy. No need to scare them," she advised.

The police were there in just a few minutes, but it felt like an hour. I was frightened while they searched the yard. Who in the world could it have been? The three of us were looking out the family room window, watching the police when Mare and Judy walked into the room.

"What's going on?" Mare said, looking concerned.

"How come the police are here?" Judy added.

"Somebody was looking in the window! They knocked over the woodpile. See?" I said as I pointed it out to them.

"Who do you think it was? A peeping Tom?" Mare asked.

Judy giggled and then said, "Ooh, how creepy!"

"Don't worry, girls, it was probably a dog, or a deer, or something like that. The police will figure it out." Mom was trying to keep us calm. Kim and I knew it wasn't an animal. We had heard footsteps and they sounded human.

The police didn't find anyone out there, but my

Mom figured out who the culprits were. After the policemen left, Mom sternly questioned them. Reluctantly, Mare and Judy confessed that they had slipped out the front door and snuck around to the kitchen window to spy on us to see what we were baking. They were hiding behind the woodpile when my clumsy sister leaned on it and pushed it over. Quickly, they ran into the house before anyone caught them. My mother wasn't very happy with those two, and neither were Kim and I. Besides scaring us out of our wits, while the police were checking outside and we were in the other room, Mare and Judy had eaten ALL of the brownies!

CHAPTER SEVEN
The Finals

By the middle of August, we had finished our league games and were into the play-offs. No one was surprised to see the Galaxies in first place, but to end up playing the championship game against the Comets was unexpected and unexplainable. How did they manage to pull it off? Not to worry though, we had beaten them before and we knew we could do it again.

So, here it was, the big day, the final game just an hour away. I was so nervous that I couldn't eat my supper. My mouth felt like it was already dry from the dust at home plate. Marianne was nervous too. I could tell by the way she was watching the clock and snapping her gum before we left for the game.

No one spoke in the car. There was no pep talk or words of encouragement from Dad tonight. I don't think he knew quite what to say in this situation, having two daughters playing against each other in a championship game.

When we arrived, the stands were packed with people. This was a big event. Marianne went over to her bench and I went over to mine. Dad stood behind the backstop, talking to another fireman in town. I wondered which side he would sit on once the game began, but I don't think he'd figured that out for himself yet.

After we warmed up for a while, the ump signaled to start the game. The Comets won the coin toss (and last ups), so we batted first.

"Good luck, Em," said Marianne and tapped me on the back with her glove as she walked by.

"Yah, good luck Mare," I replied. This was all too weird, playing the championship game against my little sister!

Marianne was playing right field and didn't look too happy about it. I played catcher of course. Lori Sullivan seemed to have permanently taken over Mare's coveted pitching position.

We were neck and neck the whole game. It must have been exciting to watch, but it was a tough one to play. We'd get a run, and then they'd get a run. We'd get them out 1-2-3, and then they'd get us out 1-2-3. It was intense, but by the end of the sixth inning, the score was Galaxies 5, Comets 4. If we could get through this last inning, we'd be the champs!

At the top of the seventh inning, we were up. Cathy struck out, and then Deb got walked to first. I hit a line drive to left field and made it on base. Our next batter was struck out easily. (Lori was pitching well). Then came Roxanne, our power hitter.

The crowd was going nuts. We now had a chance at stretching our lead to be sure to win the game. I glanced at Dad who seemed to be cheering for everybody, trying to be fair. He looked very tired. Was the sweat on his brow from the heat or from the pressure?

Smack! Roxanne took the first pitch, (though it looked a little high to me). It popped up to Marianne in right field. Mare started to run back to catch it. Meanwhile, Deb and I took off for home. Mare was never going to get it. She'd been standing too far in.

Approaching third base and watching Deb head for home, I glanced back and could not believe my eyes. Marianne jumped up in the air running, and reached out to make an impossible, perfect catch, giving us our third out!

Oooh, and she was so proud of herself! She gave me a smirk when she came in off the field. I just gave her a cold, hard stare. We were still ahead by one run and just needed three more outs to win. No problem. It was the bottom of the seventh and final inning and it was time to finish this game quick.

The Comet's first batter hit an infield pop up and was an easy out. Their second batter up struck out. This was going to be a breeze! Two up, two out. The championship was only one out away from us!

Then it was Marianne's turn to bat. She gave me that smirk of hers as she stepped up to the plate.

"Come on, Mary Beth, you can do it. No hitter here," I called out to the pitcher as I punched my fist into my glove and squatted down behind home plate. I was getting annoyed.

Marianne didn't flinch. She cocked her bat for the pitch.

Low and outside, ball one. I knew what my Dad was thinking and thought I heard him say, "Good girl, Marianne, never swing at the first pitch."

Then Mary Beth threw a beauty, but Marianne didn't bite.

"Strike one," called out the ump. I could hear her

snapping her gum. Good, the pressure was getting to her.

Next pitch looked good, too. This time she swung. I could feel the breeze, as I felt the ball land in my glove.

"Strike two!"

"Okay, M. B., take your time. One more is all we need," Coach Cushman shouted to our pitcher to help her keep her cool. She looked tired, but determined to win this game.

I signaled for a high pitch, but Mary Beth wanted to be flashy, I guess, and chose a fastball. Only problem was she missed her footing and threw wild, striking Marianne in the thigh. My sister limped a little as she walked to first base but she still had that smirk on her face.

"One more e-a-s-y out, come on guys," I called out to the team as I got in position for the next batter. But in reality, I knew we had a good hitter here.

I signaled for a low inside ball. That way, if she swung it would get hit between third and second base. Then it would be easier to make the out or at least hold up Marianne from getting any farther than second base. It was a good idea, but unfortunately, Mary Beth ignored my signal again. She must have been afraid to mess up again and took what she thought was the safe route: an easy pitch right down the middle.

Oh, and it was an easy pitch for the batter, too.

The sound was deafening as bat and ball collided followed by an eerie silence as the line drive blew by our right fielder. Marianne saw her chance and ran with all her might. She rounded third just as our right fielder recovered and threw to the second baseman. Then the second baseman threw it to me. I stood my ground at home plate, waiting to triumphantly tag her out, and win the game championship.

With the other runner not far behind her, Marianne just kept coming at me. She may be taller than me, but she didn't scare me, especially not now. With my foot firmly planted on home plate and an I-dare-you look on my face, I held up my glove to tag her. But, she didn't slow down at all. She was going to hit me full force! It seemed like slow motion as we finally made contact. In my excitement, I tagged her with my glove face open. I remembered some of Dad's advice just about then, but it was too late. I watched in horror as the ball went flying out of my glove and into the sidelines! Dad had told me so many times before: "Never tag anyone with your glove open faced. Put your other hand over the ball if you have to." It was such a basic move and I had blown it.

I couldn't watch as my sister and then the next runner scored to win the championship while I scrambled to get the ball back . . .

Final score: COMETS, 6 – GALAXIES, 5.

CHAPTER EIGHT
Friends

Oh sure, I was mad at her. Who wouldn't be in my situation? Besides, I just knew everyone was blaming me. Mary Beth had the nerve to say it was both Mare and my fault and she hated us both forever. Who cares, I didn't need poor-sport friends like her anyway. I should have told her that it was all her fault because she's a lousy pitcher and didn't listen to me, but it wasn't worth it. The season was over and the Comets had won fair and square. There was nothing we could do about it now.

It was weird at our house after the game, with my parents in the dual role of congratulating Mare and trying to cheer me up. I couldn't stand it so I decided it was easier to buck up and join in on the celebration. I had to admit it was amazing that the worst team in the league had made it from last place to first place in one season. They must have worked very hard and deserved to be in the playoffs, but I still wasn't thrilled that they won at my expense.

There was just about two weeks left until school started again. I spent a lot of time with Kim doing things like getting new clothes for school and going swimming at Lake Mark. Marianne, on the other hand, spent all her time in the garage working on her bike. It took some effort, but she did a great job. It almost looked brand new again. The yellow came off everywhere except the tires, but it looked interesting that way. At least yellow and blue go together well.

Once, I offered to help her with her project (since I had been the brains behind the scheme to paint it in the first place), but she said no thank you. She seemed to be enjoying fixing up her bike by herself.

The call came three days before school started. Marianne and I had been chosen to play on the All-Star Team! What a surprise and what an honor! The All-Star coaches picked only the best players from all the teams in the Western Mass league. With the games coming up in just two weeks, we didn't have much time to practice. But we felt ready, being so fresh out of the summer league. During those two weeks, along with All-Star practices, Dad kept us on our toes, pitching and playing catch in the evening. Practice was more enjoyable now that we were back on the same team again. Dad was happier, too.

He was also pleased about Marianne's bike, although he didn't say so... I wondered, though, if he was more pleased with Mare than he was with her bike. After all, she had cleaned it up all on her own—it was completely her idea.

It had been a long time since Mare and I had taken a ride up to Tehans store for penny candy. I really felt like going there today.

"Hey Mare," I said, "what do you say we take your bike and try out that blue color? Let's go to Tehans. Besides, we need the exercise to stay in shape for the game, right?" No argument—we were off in a flash. We even rode by Old Man Roberts' house without a second thought.

Mare was a saver and always had more money than I. She would buy the sourest candy they had. Her favorite was sour watermelon. She loved sour stuff so much she would even eat fresh-picked rhubarb with salt on it, not sugar! Just thinking about it made my mouth pucker! I, on the other hand, preferred Tootsie rolls. They fit my budget well and would be eaten before we got home. Marianne's candy would last for weeks! She seemed to have an endless supply—probably because it was too sour to eat. I never asked her to share any of it, that's for sure.

CHAPTER NINE
The Fire

Mare and I tried to get the most out of those last two weeks of summer vacation. The weather was unusually hot and made any physical activity very tiring. The All-Star coaches tried to squeeze in as many practices as possible, despite the heat. By now, Mare and I were growing tired of playing softball; it had been a softball-intense summer enough, even without getting on the All-Star team. Our team was made up of terrific players. However, a lot of us were used to doing things the way we did them on our own teams. We were all skilled players, but our big problem was learning how to work together. It wasn't easy, but we were trying the best we could.

On Friday, one week before the All-Star games, Mare and I, who usually had friends over to watch TV on Friday nights, were too tuckered out. We just hung around and did nothing. I was so tired, I went to bed early, just after dark. I was beginning to doze off when I heard my father's Fire Radio sound the alarm. Dad was off to the fire station in a flash. Sometimes these were false alarms, so I went back to bed even though I was a little curious about what kind of fire it was. But I knew Dad would tell me all about it when he got home.

Suddenly, Mare burst into my room. "Em!" she said excitedly. "Get up! Mr. Roberts' house is on fire!"

I jumped out of bed and looked out my bedroom window. Oh no! Old Man Roberts' house was on fire and there were flames shooting out the roof way up into the dark sky. I felt a chill go through my entire body.

"Come on!" Mare said. "Donna went up there with Harry to try to save Mr. Roberts!"

What? My sister Donna was there with my neighbor? I flew out of bed and joined Marianne, Joanne, and Mom running up the road to the burning house. I still had my pajamas on. Apparently, our neighbor Harry saw the fire first. He saw smoke coming out the windows, not flames. He called the fire department and then called my Dad, who was already on his way to the fire station.

My sister Donna answered the phone when he called. Harry told Donna, "I'm going up there to try to save Mr. Roberts. He's probably still in the house."

With that comment, Donna hung up the phone and ran out the door to join him, against my mother's wishes. Mom was frantic and the rest of us were scared to death. Not only were we worried about our Dad fighting the fire, now we were worried about Donna and Harry.

My lungs were aching by the time we ran up the smoky hill to the house. It was so hot that we couldn't get very close. The sound of crackling and the color of the fire-lit sky were eerie and something I will never forget.

My mother was screaming for Donna, but the sound of the fire was deafening. Donna would never hear her. Mare and I were crying. Joanne was looking around and calling her too. Donna must have gone into the burning house—we couldn't see her anywhere!

When the fire trucks arrived, we moved out of the way farther down the hill. Firemen were running everywhere, hooking up hoses, carrying axes. Two were dressed in protective suits and wearing oxygen tanks on their backs.

Others were up on ladders and chopping holes in the roof. Then the pumper truck started spraying water on the roof and into the holes. When the flames died down some, firemen broke down the front door while water was spraying around them and the two firemen wearing the special suits entered the building. I held my breath; I recognized one of those firemen as my Dad!

"DAD, DAD!" I screamed at the top of my lungs. "DONNA IS IN THERE! HARRY IS TOO!" But Dad couldn't hear me; he didn't even know we were there.

My mother looked like she was going to cry. Joanne, Mare, and I stood frozen. I felt sick to my stomach. Dad and the other fireman seemed to stay in the burning house forever. The flames were getting higher and the house was beginning to make eerie groaning noises like it was starting to fall apart. Suddenly, one of the two firemen jumped out a first floor window and fell on the ground. Was it my Dad? I couldn't tell, but Mom cried out his name.

Then the other suited fireman ran out the front door. Quickly, ambulance drivers ran over to the fallen fireman to help him. They took off his equipment to tend to him and we could see it wasn't Dad. He was the fireman who had come out the front door. The injured fireman was overcome with smoke because his oxygen tank failed. He was taken to the hospital.

Dad sat on the curb and took off his breathing apparatus. Suddenly, two people came over to him. In the darkness, harshly lit by the deadly light of the fire, we saw they were Donna and Harry! They weren't in the house after all! They had been standing on the opposite side of the hill where we couldn't see them.

What a relief! Donna, Harry, and my Dad were all safe. But what about Old Man Roberts? Looking at his house, now totally engulfed in flames and collapsing, I realized that saving him was impossible and I felt very sad.

"Dad, Dad," I cried as Dad looked across the road and saw us. We all ran over to him and Mom kissed his sooty face. "Did you find Mr. Roberts?" I asked.

Dad shook his head sadly. "No, honey, I'm afraid not. The house was filled with so much junk, huge piles of newspaper everywhere; it was a firetrap. We couldn't move around in there. We crawled on the floor and did the best we could, but no luck," he said. "After the fire is over, we'll search the house again to look for his body. He is certainly dead by now," he said sadly.

As scary and weird as Mr. Roberts was, both

Mare and I had tears in our eyes. No one deserved to die like that.

Mom gathered us all up and headed us home and Donna got an earful for running to the fire against her wishes.

"But Mom, we were just trying to save him," she said. "Besides, Harry knew just what to do. He walked up to the door and touched the doorknob. It was so hot he burned his hand. He knew better than to open it. So, we stayed away. There was nothing we could do."

"I know Donna, but we were worried sick about you. I'm thankful that you are all right. " Mom said.

When Dad came home much later that night, I could hear him and Mom talking in the kitchen. I could also smell him. Dad always came home smelling like smoke after a fire, but this time he smelled extra smoky. I knew that soon Mom would be busy washing his clothes while he took a shower. While they were chatting, I heard Dad tell Mom what happened when he entered the house. They were crawling around on the floor over all the trash and they could barely see because of the smoke. As Dad headed toward the stairs, he thought he saw Mr. Roberts lying there. He got closer and reached out to grab his arm to drag him out. As he touched what he thought was Mr. Roberts arm, he was terrified to see his head fall off and roll away! But very quickly, he saw that what he thought was Mr. Roberts was actually an old coat rack lying on the ground and the rolling head was only a pumpkin.

After an investigation, the fire marshall concluded that Mr. Roberts smoking in bed probably caused the fire. He must have fallen asleep while smoking a cigarette.

For a while after the fire, none of us rode our bikes by the site. We were too freaked out. But the day came when Mare and I finally got up the nerve. The house was nothing but charred remains, a pile of ashes and brick, and it still smelled like smoke weeks later. We stopped our bikes there for a moment, and then set off for home. As I rode down the hill, my tears were wiped away by the wind in my face.

CHAPTER T E N
All-Stars

The New England All-Star championship was held in Connecticut. We had to play two games that day, as long as we won the first one. It was unusually hot for a late September weekend. The heat was already getting to me on the ride down in the bus. We were a team made up of the best girl softball players in western Massachusetts, but we all looked as nervous as rookies. The bus was quiet except for the sound of constant gum chewing. Everybody had a mouthful of gum except Marianne. Her mouth was full of sourballs. How could she eat those things? Just the smell of them made me want to spit.

We had been forewarned that hand signals were not allowed in this playoff. It would be difficult because that's what most of us were used to, but we were ready. We were good together as a team regardless.

The first game was tough, especially with the heat, hot sun, dust, and jitters, but we pulled it off and won. Mare and I both played lousy, but everyone else picked up the slack; that's what's nice about having good players on your team.

We were all exhausted after that first game and needed a rest, but there was no time. Our next game started right away and because of the day's standings, this one would decide the championship winners. Our opponents were from Connecticut. We had never seen softball players like them before! They were huge, unfriendly, and looked a lot older than us. We weren't even sure if they were all girls. To top it off, their coach was like an army drill sergeant, yelling and screaming at his players. He was intense. They were a tight team though, and we suspected they'd been playing together all year, not like our thrown-together team. All that considered, plus it being even hotter now, we figured we were gonna get slaughtered.

We won the coin toss, but as I had feared, the game started out badly.

I was catching and Mare was in center field. The Connecticut team had first ups and scored two runs right away, which flustered our pitcher. She was giving pitches away. We finally managed to get three outs, but the damage was done. It was only the bottom of the first inning and we were behind 2 to 0.

When we got up to bat, we found out they had some impressive fielders, too. We felt like we were playing against 18-year-old boys and wished we could check their birth certificates. The only thing we had going for us was our hitting. Almost everyone managed to dig something out of the pitches we got, but our team couldn't score. No matter how we hit the ball, it went right to their fielders. They were everywhere! The first inning ended quickly.

Back on the bench, I begged the coaches to give Marianne a chance at pitching. But they barely paid attention to me. These were all-star coaches, not Mr. Cushman; they hardly knew me, never mind my sister. In that case, why would they take MY word for it? So, I went over to my dad and asked HIM to talk to the coaches, to tell them how good Mare really was. He knew everyone, but despite the look of agreement on his face, he said he didn't want to be a meddling parent. He said it was up to the coaches, not him, even though he agreed that they should put her in. I really don't know how it happened but all of a sudden, Marianne was on the sidelines, quickly warming up, and they just as quickly put her in.

It was the right decision; Marianne held them off and threw them nothing but garbage. They couldn't hit a thing. Now we had a chance at least! We weren't going to be pulverized.

Sweat pouring off my forehead, I was hitting but not getting on base, and poor Mare was a major strikeout disaster. She was swinging at anything and hitting nothing. Our coaches and parents could see what we were up against and cheered us on, but they were wilting in the heat, too. When the fickle crowd got annoyed with Mare at bat and let out a collective sigh, it made me angry. She was hot and tired like the rest of us. I wanted to tell them to give her a break. It wasn't fair. I looked over at my dad. He looked upset too, but he gave me a smile anyway, like he was trying to be optimistic or something.

The innings zipped by and it didn't take long before it was the bottom of the seventh and our last turn to bat. We were still behind 2 to 0. It was now or never.

Lyn was first to bat. She hit a fly ball and center field caught it. One out. Our next batter, Sandra, got a walk. Then Lizzy got a hit and made it on base. We now had runners on first and second. Unbelievably, the Connecticut team was starting to fall apart.

Audrey came up to bat. She was a strong hitter. Our families cheered loudly as Audrey took the first pitch and slammed it clear out to right field. She made it to first base and Sandra made it home. Now our parents were out of control.

The score was 2 to 1 and we had runners on first and second again and only one out. We needed two runs to win or one run to at least tie and go into overtime (and get another chance at winning). Laura hit, but grounded out at first base. Our runners managed to make it safely to second and third base, but now we were only one out away from the end of the game and losing.

The crowd was on their feet and everyone was screaming. They were so loud you couldn't even hear the other coach yelling orders at his team. It was Marianne's turn to bat. A huge groan came from the crowd when they realized Marianne was up next at such a crucial moment. I glanced at Dad and saw that he was steaming mad, looking around to see who it was that groaned.

Our opponents and their fans, however, were glad to see Mare coming up to bat. They thought they would win for sure now and gave a rousing cheer. They were so mean! Their coach moved his outfielders close in, anticipating an easy out to end this game. I knew Marianne had heard and seen it all and I felt terrible for her.

Knowing she really needed my help right now, I ran up to give her a pep talk. "Don't listen to them, I know you can do it Mare. Remember how you beat me in the finals? Now do that to those turkeys!" I said, pointing at their bench hoping they had heard me.

"Don't be so spastic, Em. This is gonna be a breeze," my sister said as she strolled confidently up to the plate. Huh? Bewildered by her unconcerned attitude, I went back to the bench and sat down. My little sister was up to something, and I sure hoped she knew what she was doing.

The first pitch came fast, but Mare didn't take it. Strike one, but that was okay. She was taking her time and using her head.

Mare stepped back from the plate and took a few practice swings. The other team's coach moved his outfielders in even closer! He was trying to psyche her out, but I could tell his ploy wasn't working.

"Home run hitter here," I yelled at the top of my lungs, feeling like I had to do something to help her out. People looked at me like I was crazy, but I didn't care what they thought.

She straightened her cap and stepped up to the plate again looking a little annoyed, but very determined. I knew what my sister was capable of, especially when you made her mad. Then, in that split second before she cocked her bat, my sister looked at me and winked. I knew right then and there she meant business. I was so nervous I could feel my heart pounding in my chest.

"Yah, home run hitter here!" I screamed again. This time I meant it!

The pitcher fired the ball. As it came barreling towards her, Mare's eyes locked onto it like an eagle's on its prey. I heard no noise from the crowd at all, no one was breathing. The air was still until Marianne swung through it with all her might. She nailed the ball and sent it straight over the center fielder's head. Mare ran and ran forever it seemed. By the time she made it to second base, our other two runners had scored and the game was over.

The crowd went nuts. So did the other team's coach, but he wasn't celebrating. Looking very offended, his team stormed off the field, sure to be scolded. My sister, however, was still running, focused only on scoring even though the game was over. By now, our whole team had run out to home base to celebrate, with our families right behind us.

Still, Mare kept running, and didn't stop till she found a way through the crowd to tag the plate. Her foot came down hard on the bag sending a cloud of dust up in everyone's face but no one seemed to notice.

My little sister had saved the game and we were the New England All-Star Champions!

CHAPTER ELEVEN

It Never Ends

For a summer that started out the way it did, it sure had a happy ending. Things couldn't have been better. At school, everyone was talking about the All-Star victory. Marianne was enjoying the spotlight and certainly deserved it.

One day after school, Mare and I were down at the pond, pitching stones into the water as we usually did. We weren't talking about anything in particular, but for some reason Marianne decided to tell me a secret.

"Hey Em, remember how calm I acted when I went up to bat that last time at the All-Star game?" she asked.

"Yes, I do," I answered.

"Well," she said, "I wasn't calm at all. I was so nervous my knees were shaking and I felt like throwing up."

"You sure didn't look it. Besides, we all felt that way, and it was so hot, too," I said, trying to make her forget about it.

"But that's not all," she said. "Remember when that loudmouth coach moved the outfield in again? He really made me mad! In fact, he made me so mad that I pretended the ball was him. That's why I hit it and hit it so hard!"

I cracked up. I knew the fury of Mare's anger. Even though I laughed, I must admit I was impressed; she had put her anger to good use.

"You better not tell anyone, either," Marianne

warned. I promised to keep her secret, but I was still giggling.

"You know, I was wondering, Pemps, which team are you going to sign up for next year, the Galaxies or the Comets?" my sister asked with that silly smirk on her face again.

I stopped dead in my tracks and gave her one of my own looks back. My sister was still a little stinker. She was never going to change, but that was okay with me.

ABOUT
THE AUTHOR

Though she no longer plays organized sports, Emily enjoys spending time with her kids and animals on her small farm in New England. She is the author of a variety of children's books, including the popular Mabel series (*Mabel Takes the Ferry; Mabel Takes a Sail*), and *Pumpkin Smile*. Contact her at www.emilychetkowski.com.

The author and her father.

SOFTBALL FACTS

- Softball was invented in Chicago, IL in November, 1887, at Farragut Boat Club

- 56 million Americans play at least one game of softball a year

- It is the number 1 team participant sport in the USA

- It was known as Kitten Ball until 1925

- The ball is 11 to 12 inches in circumference

- There are three types of softball: slow pitch, fast pitch, and modified pitch

- Each softball game has at least 7 innings

- The pitch must be made in an underarm fashion, and the ball must be released below the hip

- If anything happens to suspend play after 5 innings have been played, the game is ended and the score stands as it is

- The USA has the most dominant women's softball league, as they have won at the past 3 Olympics

- Softball is a descendant of baseball. The major difference is that some of the rules are eased

- The current Junior Women's World Cham pion is Japan

- There are 12 players on the field during each inning

- The game usually lasts between 1 and 2 hours

Websites used for these facts:

http://www.softball.org/about/asa_history.asp

http://en.wikipedia.org/wiki/Softball